The World of Nature

THE EVERGLADES

GALLERY BOOKS
An Imprint of W. H. Smith Publishers Inc.
112 Madison Avenue
New York City 10016

This edition first published in U.S.
in 1991 by Gallery Books,
an imprint of W.H. Smith Publishers, Inc.
112 Madison Avenue, New York, New York 10016

ISBN 0-8317-9595-6

Printed and bound in Spain

For rights information about the photographs in
this book please contact:

The Image Bank
111 Fifth Avenue, New York, NY 10003

Producer: Solomon M. Skolnick
Writer: Mark Sosin
Design Concept: Lesley Ehlers
Designer: Ann-Louise Lipman
Editor: Joan E. Ratajack
Production: Valerie Zars
Photo Researcher: Edward Douglas
Assistant Photo Researcher: Robert V. Hale
Editorial Assistant: Carol Raguso

Title page: **Bathed in early morning light, a stand of bald cypress *(Taxodium distichum)* survives in a limestone depression that holds water even during the dry season. Lily pads coat the surface, providing an essential habitat for aquatic species. *Opposite:* A pair of lofty coconut palms *(Cocos nucifera)* stand silhouetted against a typical, multi-hued Everglades sunset.**

From the southern slopes of
Florida's Central Ridge,
water flows through the
Kissimmee River Valley, Fisheating
Creek, Taylor Creek, and other
streams and joins spillover from
Lake Okeechobee to form the
fabled Everglades. Extremely
complex and diverse, this unique
habitat and ecosystem has no
parallel anywhere else in the world.
Its 10,000 square miles in southern
Florida include prairies, tree
islands, subtropical marshes, and
mangrove forests.

A river without banks spans a
width of 50 miles, easing southward
over an almost flat plain for a distance
of 100 miles from Lake Okeechobee
to Florida Bay and the Gulf of
Mexico. The gradient is so subtle
that it falls a mere two to three
inches per mile. In most places, it's
difficult to detect the water's move-
ment. Miles and miles of saw grass
(a sedge rather than a grass that
reaches a height of 10 to 12 feet and
has tiny teeth along its edges) coat
the marshy regions.

The subtropical climate
produces a wet season from June
through October and a dry season
in the winter. Rainfall averages 55
inches per year. The sheet flow of
water floods the glades when the
rains arrive and tends to disappear
during the dry season and periods
of drought.

**The strong Florida sun rises over a pine
hammock. Slash pines** *(Pinus elliottii)*
**have a thick, corky bark that insulates the
trunk against fire, a vital ingredient for
their continued survival.**

Above: The great egret *(Egretta alba)* has only white feathers and stands from 35 to 41 inches tall. *Left:* Wings spread for balance, a great egret tiptoes across a dead branch. Its diet consists of fish, frogs, lizards, and snakes. *Opposite:* The magnificent breeding plumage (called aigrettes) of the great egret nearly caused its demise in the late 1800's when hunters dramatically reduced the adult population of the birds to satisfy milliners' demands for the beautiful feathers.

Above: Stringent laws protect the great egret, but breeding pairs find themselves threatened by continued drought. Nesting occurs in colonies with other herons during the late winter and spring. *Left:* Yellow feet, black legs, and a slender, black bill make a snowy egret *(Egretta thula)* easy to spot. During the mating season, they grow breeding plumes on their backs, necks, and the top of their heads.

Right: A snowy egret feeds one of its chicks as two others wait their turn. Females lay only three or four pale blue eggs on a platform made from sticks and twigs. *Below:* Under the watchful eye of an adult, snowy egret chicks sit patiently in the nest until they grow large enough to feed on their own in the shallows. Sometime during the summer, the birds are ready to face life on their own. *Overleaf:* Water controls life in the Everglades, creating a complex food chain. Great egrets stand motionless, poised to strike passing prey. Other birds, mammals, and reptiles, including the alligator, depend on small ponds and sloughs for survival.

Water, as well as sun, wind, and even fire, serve as the lifeblood of the Everglades. Certain plants and trees, such as the South Florida slash pine and the saw palmetto, depend on fire to clear the surrounding land for new growth. Wind spreads seeds; hurricanes periodically carve changes into the landscape; water levels determine the vegetation as well as the inhabitants. Over the centuries, storm winds and tides carried many West Indian species of plants and animals to the Everglades.

Porous oolite limestone just beneath a thin mantle of marl (limestone mixed with clay) and peat (decaying plant life) form the foundation for vegetation. A rise in the limestone of one to three feet above the surrounding ground produces a hardwood hammock that remains dry throughout the year. In most areas, a hammock is teardrop-shaped with the broad end facing into the flow of water. A moat generally forms around this "island," protecting it from fire. The densely vegetated hammock might contain live oak, gumbo-limbo, mastic, royal palm, mahogany, various pines, cabbage palm, pond apple, and saw palmetto. Orchids and bromeliads also abound.

These hardwood hammocks provide a habitat for white-tailed deer, black bears, bobcats, raccoons, opossums, and endangered Florida panthers. An assortment of snakes find a haven here as well as the tree frogs and tree snails of the genus *Liguus* (found also in Hispaniola and Cuba.)

Depressions in the limestone bedrock that hold water throughout the year become a haven for dome-shaped stands of bald cypress. Unlike most conifers, bald cypresses shed their foliage in the winter. As the needles decay, they create an acid that dissolves the limestone while building the level of peat on the bottom. This process insures that the pond will survive and that the largest trees will be in the middle, thus forming the dome.

Bald eagles, as well as ospreys, hawks, and other feathered predators, perch atop the tallest cypress trees. Flocks of turkey vultures often roost in these sparse trees. On the ground, herons, egrets, wood storks, and white ibises stalk their prey in the rich, shallow waters.

Borne by the wind, willow seeds eventually settle in open ground covered with shallow water.

This page, top to bottom: Slate blue with a faint maroon hue to its extended neck, the little blue heron (*Egretta caerulea*) watches intently until a small fish ventures in range. Perfectly balanced on the lip of a board, the little blue heron strikes with incredible speed, pushing its head underwater to grab its prey. Gripping a small fish crosswise in its bill, the bird will turn its victim and swallow it head first.
Opposite: The little blue heron inhabits both the fresh and saltwater sectors of the Everglades, perching close to the water or wading in the shallows in search of food. Its relatively thick bill is grayish with a black tip; legs and feet are dark.

Above: A great blue heron *(Ardea herodias)* feeds its young on a nest of sticks. The juvenile has a darker color on the neck and head than the adult has. Nesting takes place during the winter and into the spring. *Left:* The great blue heron often stands with its head hunched on its shoulders, but when fully erect, the bird stands about four feet tall. In flight, with its neck folded and legs extended, its wingspan can reach almost six feet. *Opposite:* A solitary feeder with the ability to remain motionless, the great blue heron probes marshy areas and saltwater flats for a variety of foods including frogs, fish, reptiles, small mammals, and even other birds. Its long, tapered beak becomes a formidable weapon that strikes with incredible precision.

During the natural cycle of these trees, leaves, twigs, and other matter die, drop, and decay, building up a base of peat that rises to the surface or just above it. The willowhead then becomes a bayhead with trees that include cabbage palmetto, swamp holly, red bay, sweet bay, and cocoplum.

During the dry season, water-dependent creatures rely on the alligator to provide a habitat for them. Alligator holes are often part of a willowhead or bayhead. Using their feet and snouts, these large reptiles push back the vegetation and muck from holes in the limestone, creating oases for fish, turtles, snails, otters, and other animals that require a watery environment. Throughout the dry season, the gators keep the hole open, enabling a complex food chain to exist. Plants grow out of the muck, led by the alligator flag, a low plant that signals the site of an alligator hole. Cattail, water lily, arrowhead, pickerelweed, bladderwort, spatterdock, and spike rush are among the other plants found in this habitat.

Preceding pages: **Nestled among the prop roots of a black mangrove *(Avicennia germinans),* a green-backed heron *(Butorides striatus)* remains concealed from its enemies as it watches for food. The roots of the black mangrove are a haven for young fish and crustaceans.** *This page, top to bottom:* **Active by day as well as by night, the yellow-crowned night heron *(Nycticorax violacea)* is slate gray with a black head, orange legs, black bill, white cheeks, and a yellowish crown. Primarily nocturnal, the black-crowned night heron *(Nycticorax nycticorax)* has white breeding plumes on the back of its black head, gray wings, white underparts, and a short, thick, black bill. About the size of a crow, the green-backed heron, which actually looks more blue than green, has a chestnut head and neck and distinguishing orange or greenish yellow legs.**

Above: A Louisiana heron chick *(Egretta tricolor)* squawks for food as its nest mate waits with more patience. Also known as the tricolored heron, the mature bird has a long, slender neck and sometimes stands motionless with its bill pointing straight up. *Right:* Tricolored herons nest in colonies during the spring and summer. The chicks are ready to leave the protective domain of twigs and sticks by early fall when they begin to search on their own for frogs and fish.

Preceding page: **Known locally as the "Chokoloskee chicken" because it was often eaten by early inhabitants, the white ibis** *(Eudocimus albus)* **probes marshes, mud flats, and shoreline areas in search of crayfish and other crustaceans.** *This page, above:* **Often wrongly called a wood ibis, the wood stork** *(Mycteria americana)* **is a true stork with a gray head bereft of feathers and a long, curved, stout, black bill. Its largest known nesting colony is in Corkscrew Swamp.** *Below:* **Wood storks nest in the winter when water levels should be low, but water management by humans often disturbs required conditions.**

In the marshes, yellowish green periphyton cling to the underwater parts of plants. These sausage-like masses may contain 100 different organisms, including algae that remove calcium from the water and convert it to marl. Saw grass roots in the marl, and eventually, the dead stalks and other matter decay to form peat. The trees of bayheads and willowheads grow out of the peat, dropping more detritus, which develops acid. The acid dissolves the marl and limestone, making the cycle complete.

The pomacea or apple snail lives in this marsh. It must come to the surface of the water to breathe, which makes it vulnerable to predation by the Everglade kite. Perhaps the most specialized bird of prey in North America, the Everglade kite feeds only on the apple snail, making it totally dependent on water levels and operculate snail populations.

Everglades National Park, the third largest of the U.S. National Parks, spans the southern 2,020 square miles of the Florida peninsula. Within its boundaries, the freshwater marshes of the glades meet the mangrove forests that border Florida Bay and the Gulf of Mexico. The visitor center at Flamingo sits on land that was once

This page, top to bottom: **Two roseate spoonbills** *(Ajaia ajaja)* **face each other and spread their wings as they dance in a courtship display. Spoonbills feed in shallow water by sweeping their spatula-shaped bills from side to side, picking up shrimp and small fish. Brilliant pink birds that are more prevalent in the Everglades during the winter than in other seasons, the roseate spoonbill population continues to increase very slowly.** *Opposite:* **An anhinga** *(Anhinga anhinga)* **drying its silvery gray wings in the sun is a common sight along freshwater sloughs and ponds in the Everglades. Anhingas often swim submerged with only their long, slender necks and small heads above water.**

Above, left to right: The double-crested cormorant *(Phalacrocorax auritus)* is common along the coast as well as in the marshes. White pelicans *(Pelecanus erythrorhynchos)* begin arriving in late October from western breeding grounds and remain in the glades through the winter. *Below:* The large pouch below the massive bill of the brown pelican *(Pelecanus occidentalis)* serves to separate the fish from the water it catches and helps the bird position its prey for swallowing.

an isolated fishing village, reachable only by a marl road that became impassable when it rained. About 100 low-lying keys dot Florida Bay, a broad, shallow estuary with a maximum depth at low tide of nine feet.

A variety of mangroves grow along the coast, embracing the brackish zone that mixes freshwater with the salty bay and gulf waters. Red mangroves crowd the shorelines, easily recognizable by the maze of prop roots that battle for a toehold. Not only are they salt-tolerant, but they survive nicely with their roots totally immersed in water. Seeds take root in water-covered mud and grow. Leaves fall and decay, roots trap all types of natural and man-made debris, and eventually land forms.

Black mangroves grow on mud flats that are covered with water at high tide, but are exposed at low tide. Root projections called pneumatophores protrude from the mud beneath the trees. The white mangrove – with no distinguishing root structure – establishes itself farther from the water's edge. Buttonwood can also be found in the same area.

The mangrove wilderness, laced with rivers and creeks, ranks as a particularly rich ecosystem. The mixing zone changes both on

Above: Called a moorhen by some, the common gallinule *(Gallinula chloropus)* prefers ponds and marshes with a considerable amount of cover. The bird swims well, but tends to shy away from open water. Its primary diet includes insects, seeds, and aquatic vegetation. *Right:* The long toes of the purple gallinule *(Porphyrula martinica)* enable it to walk across aquatic vegetation as it searches for a varied diet of bugs, mollusks, seeds, beetles, dragonflies, and even small frogs. It jerks its head and tail continuously when it walks.

a seasonal basis (wet versus dry season) and over a longer period of changing weather patterns. During periods of excessive fresh water, saw grass marshes stretch closer to the coast; drought causes a salt-water incursion and the spreading of mangroves farther inland.

Mangroves form a nursery for a significant number of fish species as well as shrimp larvae. Alligators prowl this habitat in search of food. Raccoons feed on the oysters and other bounties of the sea that survive because of the mangroves. Florida Bay and its mangrove shores are the last bastion of the American crocodile (distinguished from the alligator by a narrower, pointed snout and its greenish gray color). Bottled-nosed dolphins charge into the shallows, often brushing their bodies against the prop roots of mangroves as they pursue their prey.

Manatees, or sea cows, find a haven in the canals, rivers, and backwaters of the area. These shy, harmless mammals often weigh close to a ton and reach a length of almost 15 feet. A sudden cold snap

Preceding page: **Hollow trees or abandoned woodpecker holes provide the ideal hideout for screech owls *(Otus asio)* during the day when they roost. In the Everglades, they inhabit hardwood hammocks and feed on mice, insects, and small birds.** *This page, top to bottom:* **About the size of a crow, the pileated woodpecker *(Dryocopus pileatus)*, with its red crest, black body, and white neck stripes, still manages to keep out of sight and avoid detection. The belted kingfisher *(Megaceryl alcyon)* perches high on a tree limb or wire until it spots its prey and then dives head first into the water to catch it. Chiefly nocturnal, the limpkin *(Aramus guarana)* prefers freshwater swamps and marshes where it searches for the apple snail as well as frogs, tadpoles, and aquatic insects.**

Above: With some 50 pairs of bald eagles *(Haliaeetus leucocephalus)* nesting in the southern part of the Everglades, it's not unusual to see this magnificent bird. The white head and tail feathers take four to five years to develop. *Opposite:* Most eagles nest on small keys in Florida Bay or in the mangroves along the coast. A few opt for the pinelands where they feed on small mammals and reptiles. In the air, an eagle has a relatively slow and full wing beat that appears much deeper on the downstroke than any other bird.

Left: In the Everglades, red-shouldered hawks *(Buteo lineatus)* are slightly smaller and have paler markings than do the northern representatives of their species. Nesting occurs in varied habitats that include hardwood hammocks, pinelands, cypress heads, and willow heads. *Below:* Sometimes mistaken in flight for an eagle, the osprey *(Pandion haliaetus)* is smaller and has white underparts and a brown line through its white head feathers. This hawk prefers coastal areas, but a few venture inland around ponds and sloughs. They hover at a considerable height and then fold their wings and drop on their prey, burying their talons into hapless fish. *Opposite, top:* The Everglades are the last bastion of the Eastern cougar *(Felis concolor)*, also called the Florida panther. Although they roam over a considerable territory and could be seen anywhere, most of the estimated 50 that survive seem to prefer Big Cypress Swamp and the Fahkahatchee Strand. *Bottom:* The Florida panther's fur is tawny, but the few that are seen often look grayish in dim light, particularly when the fur gets wet.

with a severe drop in water temperature can kill them, but their most dangerous enemy is a fast-moving motorboat with a propeller spinning like a buzz saw.

More than 300 species of birds have been recorded in the Everglades, including about 50 pairs of bald eagles that nest here. Ospreys, with their whistling cry, circle lazily as they wait for the precise moment to imbed their talons in a hapless fish. The Everglade kite, one of America's rarest birds, knows no other habitat. Its cousin, the daredevilish swallow-tailed kite, shows up in the spring, skimming the tops of mangroves to pick off lizards and other delectable dishes.

The anhinga (water turkey) swims underwater with incredible speed, spears its prey, and then surfaces to swallow it head first. Unlike a duck, it lacks the oil to keep its plumage dry, forcing the bird to climb up on a branch and spread its wings to dry its feathers.

Occasionally, a flock of flamingos will be seen wading and feeding in Florida Bay, a short distance from the mainland. Visitors from the Caribbean, these fabulous birds appear suddenly, linger for an undetermined period, and then disappear. The brilliantly hued scarlet ibis also puts in an

This page, top to bottom: **White feet help to identify the fox squirrel** *(Sciurus niger),* **known locally as the mangrove squirrel because it finds a home in hollow trees in mangrove marshes. Smaller than the cottontail and without white markings, the marsh rabbit** *(Sylvilagus palustris)* **can be found feeding on grasses almost anywhere in the Everglades. Masked bandits of the region, raccoons** *(Procyon lotor)* **are seldom fussy about what they eat and fare nicely in every type of habitat.**

This white-tailed deer *(Odocoileus virginianus)* appears dwarfed by the trunks of massive cypress trees as it pauses to drink at the edge of a pond. Only a few stands of these 100-year-old trees remain in the Everglades. Deer maneuver with incredible speed and agility through this marshy environment.

Above: A male river otter *(Lutra canadensis)* may grow to a length of five feet and attain a weight of 30 pounds; females are smaller. Fish make up the primary diet of this water-loving mammal that inhabits inland sloughs and ponds. *Left:* This young river otter pokes its nose out of a hollow log. Playful and intelligent animals, otters spend most of their time in the water. They swim with amazing speed and agility. *Opposite:* Although black bears *(Ursus americanus)* do live in the Everglades, they are seldom seen. *Overleaf:* A pine hammock filters the early morning sun in a drier portion of the region. Pines take root in areas where a thin mantle of humus barely covers the porous limestone. As their needles drop and decay, they create new humus, and the acids from the needles eat away at the limestone.

appearance from time to time, standing in a mangrove tree or searching for food along a shore-line. White ibises are abundant in mangrove country.

Pink roseate spoonbills probe the mud flats with their broad, flat bills, ferreting out crustaceans. The intensity of their coloration is directly related to their diet – the tiny crustaceans they eat contain red carotenoid pigments. Although considered rare, spoonbills can be found rather consistently in the Everglades.

Brown pelicans roost in the mangroves and dive for food in the shallow waters of Florida Bay. In the winter, they are joined by white pelicans that make the trek across the gulf, probably from Texas and Mexico. Wading birds seem to be everywhere. Great blue herons stand motionless on the flats, waiting for prey to come to them. The rarer great white heron can be found in the same area.

Reddish egrets excite bird watchers, particularly when they dash drunkenly across the shallows in pursuit of their prey. Whether the water is fresh, salt, or brackish, the small Louisiana heron, green heron, yellow-crowned and black-crowned night herons, common egret, and snowy egret nervously look for food.

Flocks of sandpipers, sanderlings, avocets, curlews, stilts, dowitchers, and yellowlegs, along with scores of gulls and terns, populate the exposed flats in Lake Ingraham. Black skimmers streak across the water's surface, their lower bills scooping up the daily fare.

Several species of ducks and coots can be found in the ponds and marshes. Gallinules tiptoe across the top of the aquatic vegetation. Red-shouldered hawks perch high in trees, searching for a snake or small mammal. The list of birds in residence explodes in the winter when migratory flocks arrive.

Softshell and snapping turtles live in the ponds and alligator holes, while box turtles scout the landscape. The beaches of Cape Sable attract loggerhead turtles when it's time to lay eggs. Raccoons stand by to dig up the nests and devour the eggs once they are deposited. Smaller marine turtles are also abundant in Florida Bay.

About two dozen species of snakes lurk in the Everglades, but only the rattlesnake (pygmy and

Preceding page, top: **Orchids like this one (Calopogon pulchellus) are air plants (more specifically, non-parasitic epiphytes) that grow on other plants and get nourishment from the air. Most prefer the dark recesses of hardwood hammocks and sloughs lined with cypresses. *Bottom:* Bluish purple morning glory (Ipomoea sagittata) blossoms appear during the spring and summer. This tropical vine is a hardy perennial that can be found in Mexico, Central America, the West Indies, and the Bahamas. *This page, top to bottom:* A hardy plant that requires considerable sunshine, Firewheel (Gaillardia pulchella) occupies sandy, open sites near the coast. Pink, orange, yellow, and sometimes purple blossoms of this wild flower (Lantana camara) grow together in clusters. Saw grass (Cladium jamaicensis), which can grow to be nine feet tall, is the most common plant in the Everglades.**

Preceding page, top, left to right: One of three jumping spiders in Florida, the red jumping spider *(Phidippus audax)* eats insects, doesn't make a web, and is capable of inflicting a painful bite. Holding its breath, this fishing spider *(Dolomedes triton)* climbs down a support and catches dinner by waiting underwater until a minnow or tadpole comes within range. *Bottom:* Often mistaken for the brown recluse *(Loxosceles triton)*, which has a violin marking on its head, this crab spider *(Misumena uatia)*, so named because it can move sideways, ambushes its prey and injects a poison. *This page, right:* A newly emerged monarch butterfly *(Danaus plexippus)* hangs from its empty chrysalis until its folded wings expand and it can fly away. *Below:* The spicebush swallowtail *(Pterourus troilus)* finds the right conditions around the edges of hammocks, stands of pine, or near streams. *Overleaf:* The buckeye butterfly *(Junonia coenia)*, easily identified by the two large spots on each wing, can be found on the fringes of swamps. During the summer months, most of the buckeyes in the glades belong to a West Indian species *(Junonia evarete)*, but that species mingles with a northern one in the winter.

diamondback), cottonmouth moccasin, and coral snake are venomous. The indigo snake reaches a length of eight feet, while the coachwhip attains a length of seven feet. The rosy rat snake is a constrictor that feeds on rodents.

Covering some 2,400 square miles, Big Cypress Swamp lies just to the west of the Everglades in Collier County, but it is vitally linked to the water flow of the region. Named for the bald cypress, it was once an area that supported a major logging operation. The vegetation ranges from wet prairies and saw grass marshes to hammocks of hardwoods and broad savannas. Water moving through this region supports the western part of the Everglades. Those who know the area well claim that it's difficult to tell when one leaves the glades and enters the Big Cypress.

The Fahkahatchee Strand – Fahkahatchee means "forked river" in the Miccosukee language – represents the heart of this incredible wilderness area, which covers 100,000 acres. Once almost destroyed by humans, the strand incorporates its own drainage basin to distribute rainfall. A truly wild sector, it remains a haven for wildlife species such as the Florida panther, the Everglades mink, and the wood stork. The region also

This page, top to bottom: **The American painted lady** *(Vanessa virginiensis)* **is an occasional visitor to the Everglades, particularly during the winter. An open, sunny landscape near a stream or a river attracts the American painted lady. A male zebra swallowtail** *(Eurytides marcellus)* **waits for a female to emerge from the chrysalis.** *Opposite:* **Large tree snails** *(Liguus fasciatus)* **live in the tropical hammocks of the Everglades, becoming active at night or on cloudy days. They feed on mould-like fungi growing on smooth-barked, tropical trees and they require moist, humid conditions. Similar tree snails are found only in Cuba and Hispaniola.**

Above: Less than three-quarters of an inch long, the little grass frog *(Limnaoedus ocularis)* is the smallest North American frog. Its favorite habitat is the moist, grassy edges of cypress ponds.
Left: The oak toad *(Bufo quercicus)* barely reaches an inch in length, making it the smallest toad. It lays its eggs on the bottom of shallow pools between April and September. The grayish-colored tadpoles mature in less than 90 days.

holds wild turkey, bobcat, and whitetail deer.

Corkscrew Swamp, in the northwest corner of Big Cypress, ranks as the best example of a virgin bald cypress forest remaining in South Florida, with trees reaching three to six feet in diameter. Some of these trees are over 700 years old. Now a sanctuary managed by the National Audubon Society, Corkscrew also hosts a major rookery for the wood stork.

Back in 1969, plans to build a jetport on its eastern edge vaulted Big Cypress into the international limelight and solidified its importance to the Everglades. Bulldozers almost sealed the fate of the Everglades, but a decision to abandon the project pumped new life into the entire region and helped to make the ecosystem known around the world.

South Florida's swelling population continues to threaten the fragile world of the Everglades and neighboring Big Cypress Swamp. From the air, it's easy to see the inland march of homes and businesses on both coasts as developers continue to clear land and people flock to these sectors. One factor which has saved the Everglades region from overdevelopment is the swarms of mosquitos and other biting insects which populate the area in summer.

Above: **Bright green with a white line down its side, the green tree frog *(Hyla cinerea)* measures about two inches long and feeds on insects, preferably the common fly. It lives close to water level in bushes, vines, and tree branches. *Right:* The southern leopard frog *(Rana sphenocephala)* which averages just under three inches, seldom dives into the water to escape from intruders or predators, like many other frogs do. Instead, it jumps away six to eight times so rapidly that it doesn't appear to land between jumps.**

Above: An excellent climber, the green anole *(Anolis carolinensis)*, commonly known as a chameleon because it can change color rapidly, feeds on small insects during daylight hours. *Left:* The reef gecko *(Sphaerodactylus notatus)* has the distinction of being the smallest of the geckos (up to two inches long) and the only one native to Florida. It adapts well to hammocks or beaches and feeds on small insects.

Right: The Florida redbelly turtle *(Chrysemys nelsoni)* has a reputation for spending a lot of time basking and for laying its eggs in alligator nests. This distinctive turtle grows to a shell length of 13 inches and inhabits still water with abundant aquatic vegetation (its natural food). *Below:* Unlike other softshell turtles, the Florida softshell *(Trionyc ferox)* climbs up on the bank of a pond to bask in the sun and can remain underwater for an inordinate amount of time. It grows to 20 inches and finds a home in ponds, marshes, or sloughs where it feeds on minnows, vertebrates, and invertebrates. *Overleaf:* The corn snake *(Elaphe guttata)* scales tree trunks easily to prey on birds, but it also lies in wait to ambush rodents and young rabbits. A constrictor that crushes its prey before swallowing, this inhabitant of pinelands and hammocks will coil and strike when threatened.

Left: Often found sunning on banks or overhanging vegetation, the Florida water snake *(Nerodia cyclopion)* consumes a diet of fish, frogs, and toads. It bites savagely, inflicting a serious wound on the unwary, and spurts a foul-smelling musk at the same time. *Below:* The elusive Everglades rat snake *(Elaphe obsoleta rossalleni)* reaches a length of about four feet and swims easily, often using the water as an escape route from its enemies. Its typical habitat includes saw grass, brush, and small trees. *Opposite:* The venomous pygmy rattlesnake *(Sistrurus miliarus)* seldom measures as much as 20 inches long and has rattles so small that they sound like a buzzing insect and can't be heard beyond about eight feet. They're quick to coil and strike when molested. They inhabit grassy areas close to water where they prey on frogs, lizards, rodents, and small birds.

Levees around Lake Okeechobee eliminated the natural spillover and flow of water southward years ago. The water is controlled by a network of canals. Agriculture along the northern fringes has not only sapped vital water, but added damaging chemicals to the system.

Highways that link the east coast with the west coast of Florida interfere with the normal flow of water. Although it is re-routed through culverts and canals, many question whether regulatory agencies understand as much about water as nature does. Without an adequate supply of water, the Everglades cannot survive. Habitats continue to disappear. Even now, populations of water birds have diminished dramatically. Although alligators are no longer endangered, the number of reptiles in the glades is dramatically lower than what it once was.

For those who love and appreciate the marvels of the Everglades, it's an ecosystem worth saving. Water has become a problem for the people of South Florida who periodically must endure restrictions on its use. It is not, however, a choice between water for birds or water for people, but rather a question of whether both will be able to survive on a shared water ration in an increasingly fragile land.

Preceding page: **A brown water snake (Nerodia taxispilota) gorges itself on a catfish. This largest of the water snakes swims underwater with amazing speed to capture fish, but it is also a good climber.** *This page, top to bottom:* **The color of the rough green snake (Opheodrys aestivus) blends into the vegetation, enabling it to coil around vines and branches to ambush insects. An excellent climber, the peninsula ribbon snake (Thamnophis sauritus sackeni) lives in marshes and wet prairies, where it stalks tree frogs and fishes. The nocturnal, burrowing scarlet snake (Cemophora coccinea) looks like the deadly coral snake, but has a red head instead of a black one.**

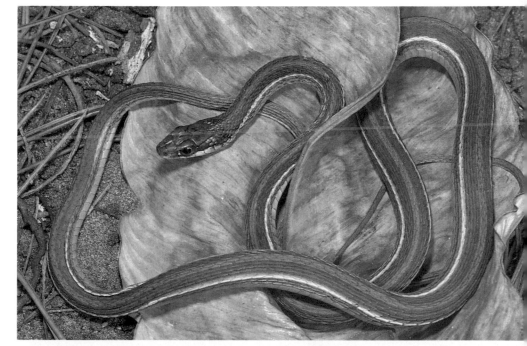

Left: Fewer than 500 American crocodiles *(Crocodylus acutus)* remain, living in brackish to salt water in Florida Bay and it estuaries. The crocodile is much more aggressive than the alligator. *Below:* The long, pointed snout, protruding teeth, and grayish color distinguish the crocodile from the alligator. Crocodiles can attain a length of 15 feet. *Opposite:* The largest recorded American alligator *(Alligator mississippiensis)* measured 19 feet, but a reptile half that length is fairly large by today's standards. The shovel-like snout with teeth set in jawbone sockets enables it to catch fish, turtles, snakes, small mammals, and birds. *Overleaf:* Found in fresh or brackish waters surrounded by a marsh or swamp, the American alligator boasts amazing speed in the water or on land. A female gator cares for its young for at least a year.

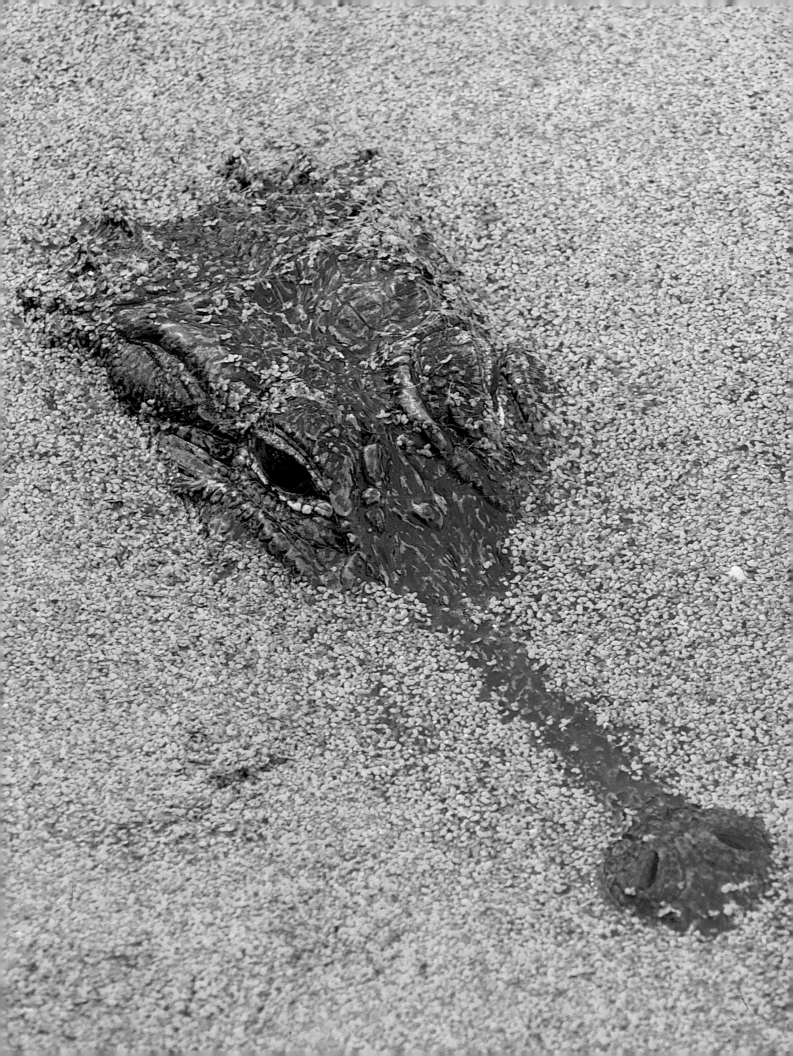

These pages: The Florida Everglades is a unique ecosystem based on the flow of water. The environment may seem harsh, but the survival of its flora and fauna depends on the very changeable supply of fresh water.

Index of Photography

TIB indicates The Image Bank